STEM ACTIVITIES LAB

Contents

The Lion King 3

Big Hero 6 29

Coco 55

The BENDON name, logo and Tear and Share are trademarks of Bendon, Ashland, OH 44805.

Copyright © 2020 Disney Enterprises, Inc. All rights reserved. Pixar Properties © Disney/Pixar

Before You Get Started

Stay safe and clean as you create. Keep your workspace clear and cover it with newspaper or cardboard. Not only does this protect your work surface, but it also makes it easy to clean up!

Gather all of your materials before starting a project. You can easily find materials for most of the projects in this book in your home, online, or at a craft or hardware store. Some projects require you to use sharp objects, hot tools, or chemicals. Ask an adult for permission and help.

© Disney

Contents

The World of *The Lion King* . . . 5

Zazu Fliers 6

Simba Mosaic 8

Pride Rock Model 10

Look at the Stars Telescope . . 13

Melting Moon Bridge Art . . . 16

Circuit Bugs 18

Rain in a Jar 22

Lioness String Art 24

The World of *The Lion King*

Simba and Nala wanted to learn about the Pride Lands outside of their home at Pride Rock. Together, they set off to explore.

Do you wonder about the world around you? Are you interested in how nature works? Explore the Pride Lands—and beyond—through science, technology, engineering, art, and math right in your own home!

Zazu Fliers

Make your own hornbill-inspired plane with straws and paper, and send the Zazu flier soaring.

Materials
- scissors
- ruler
- blue cardstock
- clear tape
- four plastic straws
- orange cardstock
- googly eyes

1. Cut two 1-inch (2.5 cm) strips from the blue cardstock along the long edge of the paper. Cut one strip in half.

2. Tape the long strip and one of the shorter strips to create two loops.

3. Cut the straws to 5 inches (13 cm) long. Make sure to cut off any bendy parts of the straws.

4. Tape one end of each straw to the inside of the larger loop, evenly spacing them around the circle.

5. Keeping the straws evenly spaced, tape the other end of each straw to the outside of the smaller loop.

6. Make a beak for your flier out of the orange cardstock. Tape it to the smaller loop. Tape googly eyes to either side of your flier.

7. Your Zazu flier is ready to soar! Try changing the length of the straws or the size of the loops to see how it affects your plane's flight.

© Disney

Simba Mosaic

Rafiki marks Simba's birth by drawing him on a tree. Design a piece of mosaic art like Rafiki's drawing of Simba.

Materials
- clear CD case
- marker
- lentils and beans of different colors
- white glue
- tweezers (optional)

© Disney

1. Open the CD case. Draw an outline of Simba's shape on one inner side of the CD case.

2. Sort the beans and lentils by shape and color. Think about creating a pattern with the lentils and beans within the Simba outline. You can also fill the area outside the outline using different colors.

3. Cover an area of the CD case with glue. Place beans and lentils on the glue. You can use tweezers to help place them.

4. Continue gluing beans and lentils to the CD case until it is covered. Let the glue dry completely. Close the CD case and display your artwork.

STEAM Takeaway

A mosaic is a decoration made of small pieces of glass, stone, or other items. Artists arrange the pieces in a design to create a work of art.

© Disney

Pride Rock Model

Pride Rock is home to Simba and the lion pride. You can build a model of Pride Rock using craft sticks.

Materials
- bamboo skewers or toothpicks
- scissors
- craft sticks of different sizes
- small items, such as coins or paper clips

4a.

1. If using bamboo skewers, get an adult's help to cut off the sharp ends. Then cut the skewers in half.

2. Using the craft sticks and bamboo skewers or toothpicks, create a bridge and towers to look like Pride Rock. Start at the base and work your way up.

3. Try different ways to create the pieces of Pride Rock. One way is to layer the sticks together.

4. Lay one stick on a flat surface. Place two sticks about 1 inch (2.5 cm) apart the opposite way, on top of the first stick so the ends overlap. Place another stick parallel to the first stick, halfway down the overlapping sticks.

4b.

© Disney

5.

5. While holding the top stick flat, weave two more sticks into the center, under the bottommost stick and over the topmost stick.

6. Add a stick underneath the last two sticks. Weave sticks on either side. Continue adding sticks and watch as the bridge forms. Add additional structures to your bridge to complete the model.

7. When your model is finished, test it by placing small items on the bridge to see if it can hold them. If it collapses, think of ways you can make your Pride Rock stronger, such as building a larger base or using a different combination of sticks. Then try again.

6a.

STEAM Takeaway

Engineering uses science to make new things. An engineer creates a design for a new object and thinks about the best materials to use. If a design doesn't work, engineers try new designs and materials. You just used engineering to create a model of Pride Rock!

6b.

© Disney

Look at the Stars Telescope

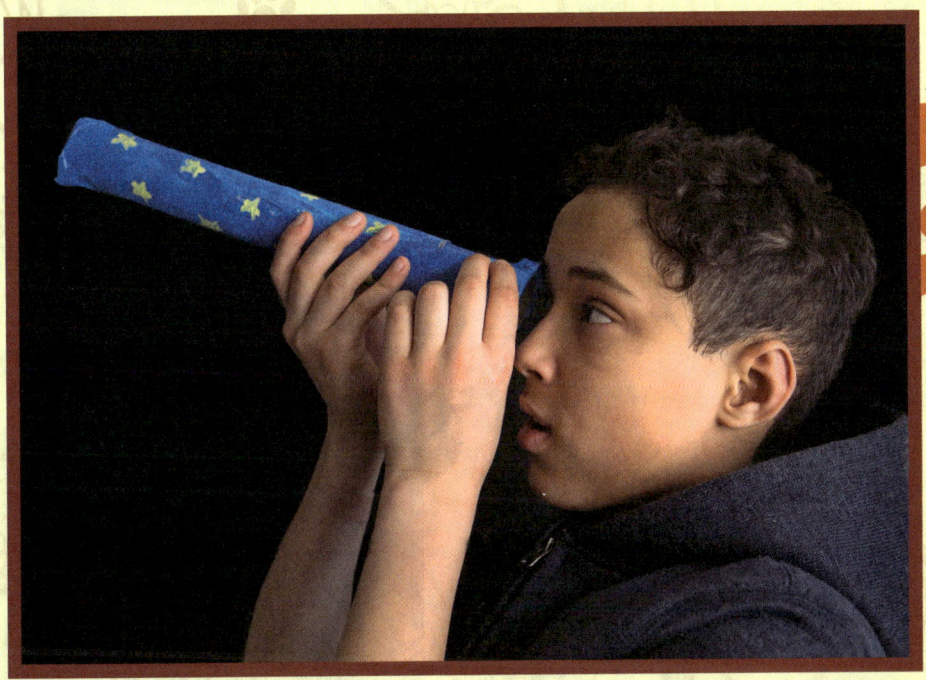

Mufasa tells Simba that the stars are always there to guide him through life. Get a better view of the stars by making a telescope.

Materials
- markers, paints, or crayons
- 2 paper towel tubes
- scissors
- lenses from a pair of reading glasses
- masking tape

© Disney

1. Decorate the outside of the paper towel tubes.

2. Cut one of the paper towel tubes lengthwise. Roll the tube so the cut sides overlap and the tube is smaller in width than the uncut tube. Place one end of the rolled tube inside the uncut paper towel tube. Adjust how tightly the inside tube is rolled until it slides in and out smoothly.

3. You can find reading glasses at the dollar store, or ask an adult for permission before using an old pair of glasses. Have an adult help you push out the lenses.

1.

2a.

2b.

STEAM Takeaway

The lenses help more light reach your eye. They bend the light, making what you see appear larger. Different lens curves can change the size of the image you see. Changing the reading glasses lenses can change how your telescope works.

© Disney

4. Tape one lens to the end of the inside tube. The lens should curve to face inside the tube.

5. Tape the second lens to the outside tube at the other end of the telescope. This lens should curve to face away from the tube.

6. To view the stars or something far away, look through the lens of the inside tube. Find something in the distance, and use your telescope to make it appear closer. To focus your telescope, slide the outside tube in or out.

4.

5.

Melting Moon Bridge Art

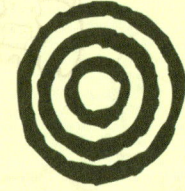

Timon and Pumbaa help Simba learn to live life with fewer worries. Use old crayon bits and heat to create carefree, moonlit artwork of the three friends.

Materials
- old crayons
- small white poster board
- pencil
- blue painter's tape
- white glue
- hair dryer
- black permanent marker

© Disney

1. Remove paper wrappers from the crayons. Break crayons into small pieces.

2. On the poster board, draw the outline shapes of Simba, Pumbaa, and Timon walking across the log bridge in front of the full moon.

3. Cover the moon with painter's tape.

4. Glue pieces of crayon in a line across the top of the poster board. Let the glue dry completely.

5. Prop the poster board up so it is standing upright. Put newspaper or another covering under it because the crayons drip off the board as they melt. With help from an adult, blow hot air from the hair dryer over the crayons until they melt and start to run.

6. Angle the hair dryer so the crayons drip down the white areas of the poster board. Continue until most of the poster board is covered with melted crayon. While the melted crayon is still warm, remove the painter's tape. Let the poster board cool.

7. Use the black marker to color in Simba, Pumbaa, Timon, and the log.

© Disney

Circuit Bugs

When Simba joins Timon and Pumbaa, he learns the slimy yet satisfying joy of eating bugs. Create your own creepy-crawly bug that actually moves.

Materials
- scissors
- toothbrush
- double-sided foam tape
- small vibrating motor
- coin cell battery
- pipe cleaner
- googly eyes

© Disney

1. Have an adult help you cut off the handle of the toothbrush.

2. Cut a piece of foam tape to fit the toothbrush head. Stick one side of the tape to the back of the toothbrush head.

3. Attach the motor to the other side of the foam tape, leaving room on one side of the tape for the battery.

4. Place one wire from the motor on the foam tape. Place the battery on top of the wire, pressing it down hard to secure it to the tape.

© Disney

5. Cut another small piece of tape. Attach it to the end of the other wire.

6. Tie a pipe cleaner around the center of the toothbrush head, and cut it to act as antennas. Attach googly eyes to the front of your bug.

6a.

6b.

7. When you are ready to see your circuit bug move, place the exposed end of the wire between the pipe cleaners and the battery. Hold the wire in place with the foam tape you placed on the end. The wire must touch the battery to turn the bug on.

STEAM Takeaway

Your bug uses a motor and a battery to move. When you connect the motor to the battery, you create an electrical circuit. This makes the motor run, which causes the toothbrush head to vibrate and move.

Rain in a Jar

During the drought, food is hard to find near Pride Rock. Rain is necessary for animals to drink and plants to grow. Create your own rainstorm in a jar.

Materials
- large clear jar
- water
- blue food dye
- small dish
- shaving cream foam
- plastic dropper

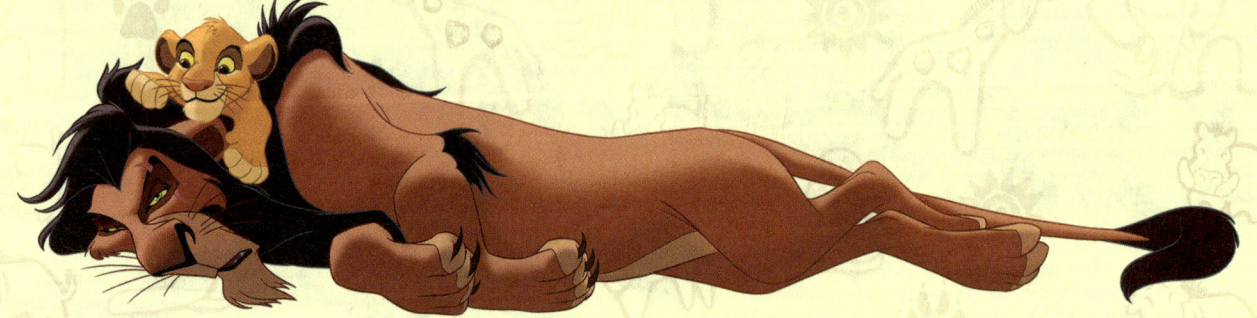

© Disney

1. Fill the jar with water, about 1 inch (2.5 cm) from the top.

2. Mix together 5 drops of blue food dye and 2 tablespoons of water in a small dish.

3. Spray shaving cream foam to fill the jar opening.

4. Using the dropper, carefully drop the blue water onto the shaving cream. Watch as the blue "rain" fills the "cloud" and then enters the jar.

STEAM Takeaway

Water vapor in the sky sticks together to form clouds. When drops of water in the clouds get heavy enough, gravity pulls the drops down as rain. The falling drops are denser than the clouds. In your jar, gravity pulls the blue "raindrops" down through the shaving cream "cloud."

© Disney

Lioness String Art

Nala and the lionesses help Simba fight Scar at Pride Rock. You can make a roaring lioness for your wall.

Materials
- pencil
- square wood block
- small finishing nails
- hammer
- scissors
- string or embroidery floss in several colors

© Disney

2.

1. Draw an outline of Nala or your favorite lioness on the wood block.

2. With an adult's help, place nails ½ inch (1.3 cm) apart along the outline and use the hammer to pound them into the wood. Leave at least ½ inch of each nail sticking out from the wood block.

3. Cut a long piece of string or embroidery floss. Tie the string to one nail.

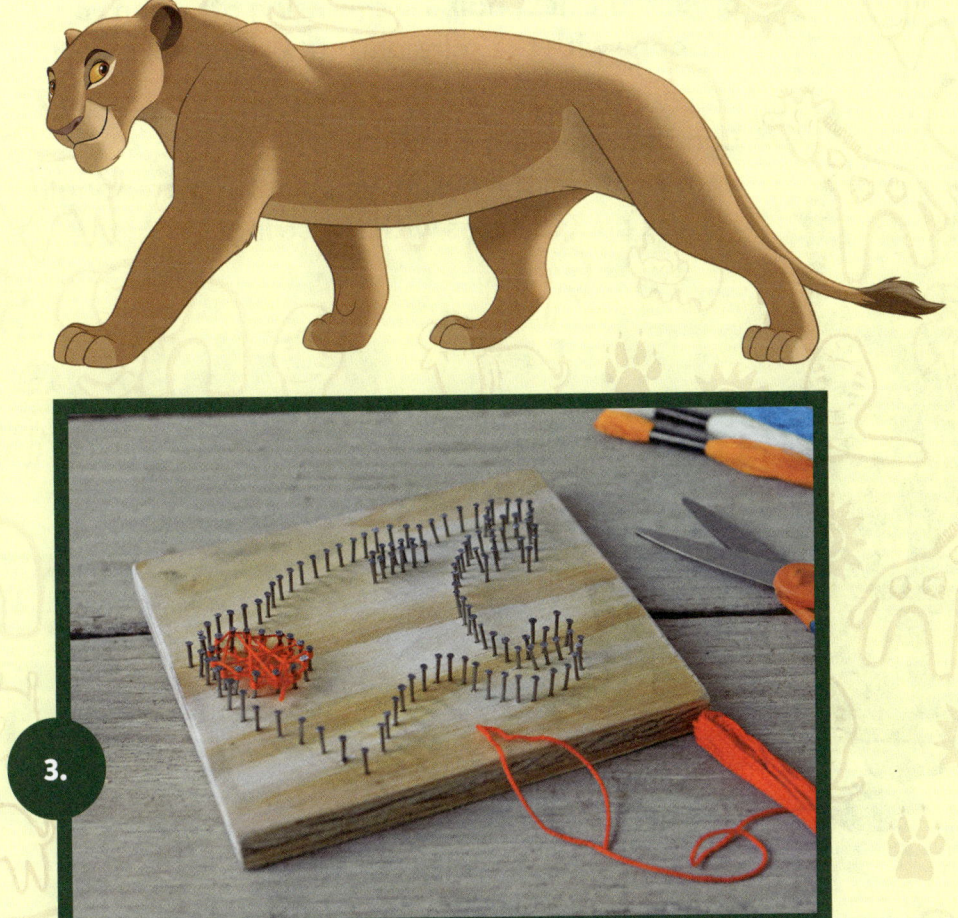

3.

4. Weave the string between the nails to create a pattern. Pull the string tight when you wrap it around the next nail. Tie the string off when you are done with the color and cut off any excess.

5. Continue weaving string of different colors until you have the design you want. Try creating shapes and patterns with the string!

© Disney

5.

The photographs in this book were created by Shaina Olmanson.
Special thanks to hand models Miles Stuart, Oliver Tran, Kjell Olmanson, and Magnus Olmanson.

Copyright © 2020 Disney Enterprises, Inc. All rights reserved.

No part of this book may be reproduced, stored in a retrieval system, or transmitted in any form or by any means—electronic, mechanical, photocopying, recording, or otherwise—without the prior written permission of Lerner Publishing Group, Inc., except for the inclusion of brief quotations in an acknowledged review.

Lerner Publications Company
A division of Lerner Publishing Group, Inc.
241 First Avenue North
Minneapolis, MN 55401 USA

For reading levels and more information, look up this title at www.lernerbooks.com.

Main body text set in Mikado a 14/18.
Typeface provided by HVD Fonts.

Library of Congress Cataloging-in-Publication Data

Names: Olmanson, Shaina, author.
Title: The Lion King idea lab / by Shaina Olmanson.
Description: Minneapolis, MN : Lerner Publishing Group, Inc., [2020] | Series: Disney STEAM projects | Includes bibliographical references and index. | Audience: Ages 7–11. | Audience: Grades K to 3.
Identifiers: LCCN 2018054257 (print) | LCCN 2018055350 (ebook) | ISBN 9781541561595 (eb pdf) | ISBN 9781541554856 (lb : alk. paper) | ISBN 9781541574045 (pb : alk. paper)
Subjects: LCSH: Handicraft—Juvenile literature. | Science—Experiments—Juvenile literature. | Lion King (Motion picture)—Juvenile literature. | Africa—Social life and customs—Juvenile literature.
Classification: LCC TT160 (ebook) | LCC TT160 .O46 2020 (print) | DDC 745.5—dc23

LC record available at https://lccn.loc.gov/2018054257

Manufactured in the United States of America
1-45803-42685-3/29/2019

Photo Acknowledgments

Additional image credits: E_K/Shutterstock.com (gears); Belozersky/Shutterstock.com (flask); Aksenova Natalya/Shutterstock.com, p. 6 (glue); Olga Kovalenko/Shutterstock.com, p. 6 (scissors); Richard Sharrocks/Getty Images, p. 7 (crayons); SJ Travel Photo and Video/Shutterstock.com, p. 7 (paints).

© Disney

Contents

The Incredible Teamwork of *Big Hero 6* *31*

Cityscape Array 32

Go Go Tomago Spinner 35

Mixed-Up Goo 37

Magnetic Sculpture 39

Jumping Magnets .... .41

Lemon Balloon 44

Bouncing Bubbles 46

Laser Rainbow 48

Solar Oven 50

The Incredible Teamwork of *Big Hero 6*

Hiro and the Big Hero 6 team create clever inventions to protect San Fransokyo. They build robots, mix up strange chemistry experiments, and work with powerful lasers in their lab to become high-tech crime-fighting team. Supervillains don't stand a chance!

Explore San Fransokyo and the world of *Big Hero 6* with fun science, technology, engineering, art, and math projects.

© Disney

Cityscape Array

Big Hero 6 must save San Fransokyo from Yokai. Use your design skills to create a San Fransokyo cityscape.

Materials
- pencil
- construction paper in at least 2 different colors
- ruler
- scissors
- glue stick
- pair of dice (optional)
- markers

1. **Draw tall city buildings in different shapes and sizes on construction paper. A ruler can help you make straight lines. Cut out the buildings.**

2. **Glue the buildings in a row on a large sheet of construction paper of a different color.**

3. **Cut at least four small squares of construction paper. The squares should be a different color from the buildings.**

4. Glue the squares onto a building in an array. An array is objects arranged in rows and columns. For example, a 2 × 2 array would have two rows of windows with two columns in each row.

5. Choose different arrays for the other buildings. Try rolling two dice to get the row and column numbers for the arrays. Cut out more small paper windows, and glue them to the buildings.

6. San Fransokyo was inspired by Tokyo and San Francisco. Use the two real cities as inspiration to add designs to your San Fransokyo cityscape with markers. You can hang it up in your room like a poster!

Go Go Tomago Spinner

Go Go Tomago fights evil with fast-spinning discs. You can design a colorful disc that will spin on a looped string.

Materials
- pencil
- drinking glass
- cardboard
- scissors
- markers
- hole punch (optional)
- string

1. Use a pencil to trace a circle around a drinking glass on a piece of cardboard. Cut out the circle. This will be your spinning disc.

2. Use markers to decorate the disc with colorful designs.

3. Carefully use the pencil or hole punch to make two holes near the center of the disc, about ½ inch (1.2 cm) apart.

4. Cut a piece of string 36 inches (0.9 m) long.

5. Thread one end of the string through both punched holes. Then tie the ends of the string together, forming a loop.

6. Hold one end of the loop in each hand with the disc in the center. Twist the looped string by making small, quick circles with your hands in the same direction. The string should start twisting on either side of the disc.

7. When the string is twisted almost all the way to your hands, repeat stretching your hands apart and bringing them together. If the string is twisted tightly, the disc will spin like a fan.

8. When your string unwinds, repeat steps 6 and 7 and try again.

1.

2a.

2b.

5.

Mixed-Up Goo

Mix up a playful substance like one that Honey Lemon might create in the lab.

Materials
- 1 cup water
- large bowl
- 2 cups cornstarch
- food coloring
- spoon (optional)

1. Slowly pour the water into the bowl.

2. Carefully add the cornstarch to the water.

3. Add 2 to 3 drops of food coloring to the water and cornstarch mixture.

4. Use a spoon or your hands to stir the mixture gently to form goo.

5. Pick up the goo. Does it stay together like a solid or spread out like a liquid? Next, roll the goo into a ball and see if it acts like a solid or a liquid. Try different things to see how the goo reacts.

STEAM Takeaway

The mixed-up goo is a non-Newtonian fluid. Non-Newtonian fluids can behave like liquids or solids depending on the forces acting on them. When the goo is at rest, it behaves like a liquid. When a force such as the motion created by your hands acts on the goo, it behaves like a solid.

Magnetic Sculpture

Hiro's microbots join together to form useful structures. Use metal parts and magnets instead of microbots to build a sculpture.

Materials
- metal lid from a jam or mason jar
- 4 to 6 hobby magnets
- 10 to 15 nuts, bolts, and washers
- a few paper clips or small metal pieces

© Disney

1. Set the metal lid on a tabletop.

2. Attach a hobby magnet to the surface of the lid.

3. Place nuts, bolts, washers, and other metal bits, such as paper clips, on the magnet to create a sculpture.

4. Add more magnets to make the sculpture taller or wider.

5. Continue to add metal bits around the magnets to create a design that you like. You can make your sculpture stand tall or spread it out along the lid.

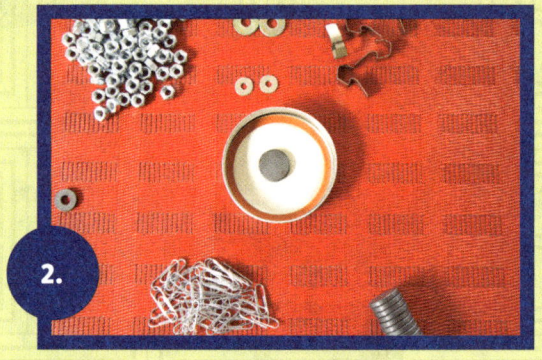

2.

3.

4.

STEAM Takeaway

A sculpture is a form of 3-D art. A relief sculpture projects from a background and often hangs on a wall. A sculpture in the round stands freely on a base, like many statues. Your magnetic sculpture can be relief or a sculpture in the round depending on how you build and display it.

© Disney

Jumping Magnets

Go Go Tomago uses magnetic force to move high-speed wheels. You can use the same force to make magnets jump and move without touching them.

Materials
- drinking straw
- clothespin
- 3 or more disc magnets with holes

1. Place the straw upright on a table or countertop. Clip the clothespin to the bottom of the straw, and grasp the clothespin to hold the straw in place.

2. With your other hand, place one disc magnet onto the straw so it slides down.

3. Add another disc magnet to the straw. If the top magnet attaches to the bottom magnet, remove the top magnet and turn it over. Flipping it turns its magnetic poles. Drop it onto the straw again. The magnets will push away from each other instead of pull together.

4. Slide the bottom magnet up the straw, and watch the top magnet move without anything touching it.

5. You can add more magnets to the straw and watch how they jump and move when you slide the bottom magnet upward.

STEAM Takeaway

Magnets have a north pole and a south pole. The pole of one magnet is attracted to the opposite pole of another and pushes away from the same pole. So a magnet's north pole is attracted to the south pole of another magnet, but two north poles push away from each other.

Lemon Balloon

Honey Lemon uses chemical reactions to help make the world a better place. Chemistry can help you use a lemon to inflate a balloon.

Materials
- kitchen funnel
- empty plastic water bottle
- 3 ounces (⅓ cup) lemon juice
- uninflated balloon
- 2 tablespoons baking soda

1. Hold the kitchen funnel above the water bottle, and pour the lemon juice.

2. Rinse and dry the funnel.

3. Hold the balloon so its opening is facing upward, and place the narrow end of the funnel in the opening. Pour the baking soda into the funnel, allowing the baking soda to fall into the balloon.

4. Making sure you keep the baking soda in the balloon, carefully wrap the opening of the balloon around the lemon juice bottle's opening.

5. Slowly tip the balloon up to allow the baking soda to fall into the bottle and mix with the lemon juice.

6. Watch the balloon inflate!

STEAM Takeaway
Lemon juice mixed with baking soda causes a chemical reaction. When they interact in the bottle, they create a gas called carbon dioxide. This gas inflates the balloon.

1.

3.

4.

© Disney

Bouncing Bubbles

Baymax the personal health-care robot can bounce. Blow bubbles that bounce on your hand.

Materials
- 1 cup distilled water
- bowl
- 3 ounces (⅓ cup) liquid dish soap
- drinking straw or pipe cleaner
- 1 teaspoon shampoo
- knit winter glove

© Disney

1. Pour the distilled water into a bowl.

2. Add the dish soap, and gently stir with your straw or pipe cleaner.

3. Add the shampoo to the water to help the bubbles last longer.

4. Put a knit winter glove on one hand.

5. If you're using a straw, dip one end of the straw into the liquid. Gently blow a bubble through the dry end of the straw. If you have a pipe cleaner instead, shape an end of the pipe cleaner into a dime-size circle. Twist the end to seal the circle, and dip it into the liquid. Gently blow a bubble through the circle.

6. Try to catch the bubble on your gloved hand. The glove's soft fabric allows the bubble to bounce.

© Disney

Laser Rainbow

Wasabi uses lasers to make precise slices. Point a flashlight like a laser, and use it to create a rainbow light show.

Materials
- clear glass jar
- water
- flashlight
- reused compact disc (CD)
- masking tape

1. Fill the glass jar halfway with water. Set the jar on a surface near a wall.

2. Hold the flashlight so the handle is parallel with the wall. Point the flashlight at the jar so light shines through the water and out the opposite side. Set the flashlight down, leaving the light on to shine through the jar.

3. Lean the CD against the opposite side of the jar from the flashlight, so it faces the flashlight. Angle the CD until a rainbow appears on the wall. Tape the CD to the jar to hold it in place.

4. Try making new rainbow designs by adjusting the positions of the jar, flashlight, and CD.

STEAM Takeaway

Tiny ridges on the CD cause light to split into different colors, forming a rainbow. Water causes light to bend, which also separates the colors and forms a rainbow.

Solar Oven

Aunt Cass makes delicious food at the Lucky Cat Café. You can build an oven that heats food using the sun's energy.

Materials
- shallow cardboard box like a clean pizza box
- markers
- ruler
- scissors
- glue stick
- aluminum foil
- black construction paper
- clear plastic wrap
- masking tape
- marshmallows
- 2 sticks
- graham crackers
- chocolate bar

1. Place the closed box with its hinge facing away from you. Start near the back-left corner, and draw a long line 1 to 2 inches (2.5 to 5 cm) from the box's edge. Keep going until you draw three sides of a rectangle, stopping near the back-right corner.

2. With an adult's help, cut along the line to create a door flap.

3. Decorate the outside of the box with markers.

4. Glue a sheet of aluminum foil, with the shinier side facing up, to the inside of the door flap.

5. Glue a sheet of black construction paper to the inside bottom of the box.

6. Stretch clear plastic wrap across the door flap's opening, and tape it in place. Your solar oven is ready!

7. Place a few marshmallows inside the oven near the middle of the black paper, and close the box top.

© Disney

8. Take your oven to an unshaded space outside. Make sure it is a warm and sunny day! Set your oven to face the sun, and prop the door flap open with sticks at the sides. Adjust the flap and sticks until the aluminum foil reflects sunlight into the box. Then tape the sticks in place.

9. Wait 1 to 2 hours for the marshmallows to heat up. Try serving them between two graham crackers with a small piece of chocolate to make s'mores.

STEAM Takeaway

Solar ovens work by focusing heat from the sun. Aluminum foil reflects sunlight into the box that is absorbed by the black paper. The paper heats up and warms the air above it. Plastic wrap traps the warm air in the box, heating the marshmallows. Yum!

To Ms. Erin Becerra, Ms. Flo Yssel, and Ms. Rachel Finney, who inspire innovation in STEAM by seeing and loving children first

Photo Acknowledgments

Additional image credits: Belozersky/Shutterstock.com (flask); E_K/Shutterstock.com (gears); Aksenova Natalya/Shutterstock.com p. 6 (glue); Olga Kovalenko/Shutterstock.com, p. 6 (scissors); Gina Djumlija/EyeEm/Getty Images, p. 7 (paper); SJ Travel Photo and Video/Shutterstock.com, p. 7 (paints).

Copyright © 2020 Disney Enterprises, Inc. All rights reserved.

No part of this book may be reproduced, stored in a retrieval system, or transmitted in any form or by any means—electronic, mechanical, photocopying, recording, or otherwise—without the prior written permission of Lerner Publishing Group, Inc., except for the inclusion of brief quotations in an acknowledged review.

Lerner Publications Company
A division of Lerner Publishing Group, Inc.
241 First Avenue North
Minneapolis, MN 55401 USA

For reading levels and more information, look up this title at www.lernerbooks.com.

Main body text set in Mikado a 14/18.
Typeface provided by HVD Fonts.

Library of Congress Cataloging-in-Publication Data

Names: Ahrens, Niki, 1979- author.
Title: Big Hero 6 idea lab / Niki Ahrens.
Other titles: Big Hero six idea lab
Description: Minneapolis : Lerner Publications, [2020] | Series: Disney STEAM projects | Includes bibliographical references and index. | Audience: Ages 7–11. | Audience: Grade 4 to 6.
Identifiers: LCCN 2018050613 (print) | LCCN 2018051945 (ebook) | ISBN 9781541561557 (eb pdf) | ISBN 9781541554825 (lb : alk. paper)
Subjects: LCSH: Handicraft—Juvenile literature. | Science projects—Juvenile literature. | Superheroes—Juvenile literature. | Big Hero 6 (Motion picture)—Juvenile literature.
Classification: LCC TT160 (ebook) | LCC TT160 .A33 2020 (print) | DDC 745.5—dc23

LC record available at https://lccn.loc.gov/2018050613

Manufactured in the United States of America
1-45800-42682-2/15/2019

© Disney

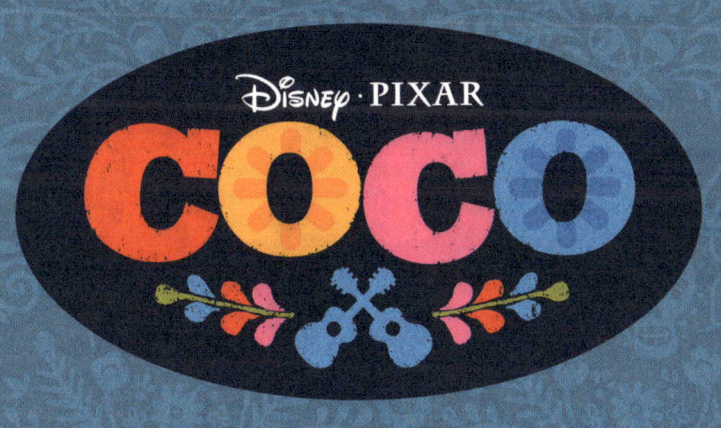

Contents

The Magic of *Coco* 57

Papel Picado 58

Pistachio Marigolds 62

Cereal Box Guitar 65

Walking Water Bridge 69

Disappearing Bones 72

Cactus Self-Portrait 73

Wing-Flapping Alebrije 76

The Magic of Coco

Miguel set out to discover the mysteries behind his family's story and ended up on a magical journey. Día de los Muertos is Spanish for "Day of the Dead." On this holiday, people celebrate and remember friends and family members who have passed away.

Connect science, technology, engineering, art, and math to the traditions of Día de los Muertos and *Coco*'s Land of the Living and Land of the Dead.

Papel Picado

A papel picado banner is folded and cut to reveal a design. Create your own papel picado banner to decorate for holidays and celebrations, including Día de los Muertos.

Materials
- solid-colored tissue paper in at least 2 colors
- ruler
- scissors
- hole punch
- white glue
- twine or string, about 75 inches (191 cm) long

1. Cut the tissue paper into 10 even rectangles, about 6 inches (15 cm) high and 7 inches (18 cm) wide.

2. Fold over one edge of the long side by about a ½ inch (1 cm). Make a crease.

3. Turn the paper so the folded edge is on the left. Fold the paper in half toward you. Fold it into thirds in the same direction.

4. On the end opposite your first fold, cut off the corners to create a half circle.

5. Unfold the paper until it is only folded in half.

6. Fold it in half the other direction, bringing the scalloped edge to the edge with your very first fold. Turn your paper so the scallops are at the bottom edge.

© Disney

7. Take the bottom right corner of the paper and bring it up to the top side to create a wedge. Repeat the fold, bringing the new bottom right corner up to the top side again to create a smaller wedge shape.

8. Cut a little off the sharp tip at the bottom of your folded paper. On either side of the tip, cut a half petal shape from the edge.

9. Unfold the paper once. Directly across from the center petal shape, punch some holes. If there is room, try punching the holes in a diamond shape.

10. Open the paper to see the design. Repeat with all sheets of tissue paper. You may wish to experiment with creating different designs.

11. Open each paper, and put a thin line of glue inside the center of the top fold. Place the string on the glue, and fold the paper over the string. Press along the crease.

12. When the glue dries, you're ready to hang your banner!

© Disney

Pistachio Marigolds

Bright orange marigolds guide Miguel's ancestors to the family's ofrenda, or offering. Make your own marigolds using leftover pistachio shells.

Materials
- 30 pistachio shells for each flower
- low-temperature hot glue gun
- hot glue sticks
- orange acrylic craft paint
- small paintbrush

1. Rinse the pistachio shells, and let them dry.

2. Glue 3 pistachio shells together. The bowl-shaped sides will face in to create the center of the flower.

3. Place a drop of glue at the base of one shell. Press the shell to the center grouping of shells. Continue to glue the shells one at a time around the center to build the flower. Create at least 3 rings of petals. Allow the glue to cool completely.

4. Paint the marigold orange. Let it dry before displaying. Create more marigolds if you have extra pistachio shells!

Cereal Box Guitar

Use recycled boxes and rubber bands to make a guitar like Ernesto de la Cruz's.

Materials

- scissors or craft knife
- 1 empty spaghetti box or long, rectangular box of similar size
- white glue
- white card stock
- 1 empty cereal box
- small screwdriver
- low-temperature hot glue gun
- hot glue sticks
- cardboard scraps
- 6 extra-large rubber bands
- markers

© Disney

1. Cut the spaghetti box so it is 5 inches (13 cm) long. Glue card stock to cover it and the cereal box. Cut a large circle from the lower half of the cereal box.

2. With an adult's help, use the screwdriver to punch 6 evenly spaced holes on the cereal box 2.5 inches (6 cm) from the bottom of the circle. At the top of the spaghetti box, punch 6 evenly spaced holes.

3. Glue the cereal box closed. Glue the cut side of the spaghetti box to the top of the cereal box. This will be the guitar's neck.

4. **Make the nut and the bridge for your guitar's strings.** Cut 4 pieces from the cardboard scraps ½-inch (1 cm) high by 3 inches (8 cm) long. Stack and glue two pieces together. Repeat. Glue one cardboard piece about 2 inches (5 cm) below the circle, above the screwdriver holes. Glue the other piece about 1 inch (2.5 cm) from the top of the guitar's neck.

5. **Cut the rubber bands.** Knot one end of each rubber band, and lace them through the holes near the bottom of the guitar.

6. **Feed the other end of each rubber band through the guitar's top holes.** Knot the ends to hold them in place.

7. Using the hot glue gun, glue the spaghetti box closed. Use markers to decorate the guitar.

8. Press the strings on the neck while you strum your guitar to make different notes.

STEAM Takeaway

A guitar string vibrates when it is plucked, causing the air around the string to move away. The air inside the guitar also vibrates, and this creates a sound.

© Disney

Walking Water Bridge

The marigold bridge connects the Land of the Dead to the Land of the Living. Science will help you create a colorful bridge on your table.

Materials
- 7 pint-size mason jars or clear glasses
- water
- red, yellow, and blue food coloring
- 6 paper towels

1. Place the jars in a line. Fill every other jar with water, 1 inch (2.5 cm) from the rim of the jar, so 4 jars have water.

2. For the water jars: Place 10 drops of red food coloring in the left jar. In the next jar, place 5 drops of red food coloring and 10 drops of yellow food coloring. In the next jar, place 15 drops of yellow food coloring. In the last jar, place 10 drops of blue food coloring.

3.

3. Fold the paper towels the long way into strips. Place one end of a paper towel in the red water and the other end in the empty jar next to it. Then place one end of the next paper towel in the empty jar and the other end in the orange water next to it. Continue with the remaining jars and paper towels.

4. Watch as the colored water travels up the paper towels and then down into the empty glasses to create a vibrant bridge.

STEAM Takeaway

The liquid water particles tend to stick together, so they pull one another across the paper towels from the full jars to the empty jars.

Disappearing Bones

In *Coco*'s Land of the Dead, souls disappear, along with their bones, when they are forgotten. In the Land of the Living, you can make "bones" disappear too.

Materials
- scissors
- 1 or 2 foam cups
- acetone nail polish remover
- 1 pint-size mason jar
- rubber gloves

1. Cut bone shapes from the foam cups.

2. Have an adult pour acetone into the mason jar.

3. Put on the rubber gloves.

4. Carefully place the foam bones in the jar. Watch as they disappear!

STEAM Takeaway
The acetone dissolves the chemicals that hold the foam cup together, making the bones seem to disappear. If you drain the acetone from the jar, in the bottom you will find a piece of plastic that is left over from the foam.

Cactus Self-Portrait

During the Sunrise Spectacular, Frida Kahlo's dancers climb an enormous cactus that looks a lot like her. You can grow your own cactus hair from tiny seeds.

Materials
- acrylic or tempera paint
- paintbrushes
- 2 small pots with drainage holes, 3 inches (8 cm) tall
- cactus soil
- baking dish
- oven
- water
- small dish to hold both pots
- at least 6 cactus seeds
- large zip-top sandwich bag
- tray

© Disney

1. **Paint each pot, and allow it to dry completely. Paint your pot to look like Frida Kahlo. (The cactus will be the hair.) If you need help deciding how to decorate your pots, research Frida Kahlo in a book or have an adult help you learn more online.**

2. **Wash your hands before touching the materials. Sterilize the soil by baking it in the oven at 300°F (149°C) for 30 minutes. Let it cool before using.**

3. **Wash and dry each pot before planting. Fill both pots with soil, pressing down lightly.**

4. **Place a few inches of water in the small dish. Then place both pots in the water. Wait a few minutes until the soil is soaked.**

6.

5. Place the seeds on top of the soil in both pots. Sprinkle a small amount of soil over the top of the seeds, no more than ⅛ teaspoon for each pot.

6. Lift one pot from the water, and place it in the zip-top bag. Repeat with the second pot. Seal the bag and place it on a tray near a sunny window.

7. Your cactus seeds should start to sprout in 3 to 7 days. You can open the bag when you see the first spines.

STEAM Takeaway

Frida Kahlo (1907–1954) was a Mexican artist known for her self-portraits that blended real life and fantasy. She used symbolism and elements of Mexican folk art to paint her stories.

Wing-Flapping Alebrije

Alebrije figurines often resemble everyday animals with fantastical elements. Make a model with moving wings inspired by alebrijes.

Materials

- oven-bake polymer clay
- paper clips (optional)
- 1 old baking sheet
- oven
- tempera or acrylic paint
- paintbrushes
- cotton swabs or toothpicks (optional)
- 1 sheet thick card stock
- craft glue
- scissors
- 2 plastic straws
- thick string or yarn
- 1 chopstick (optional)

© Disney

1. Mold the clay into a fantastical figure. Be sure to leave a 1-square-inch (6.4 sq. cm) surface on the back or sides of your animal for each wing. You can use paper clips to attach design pieces and limbs to the figure's body.

2. Place your figure on the baking sheet. Bake according to the clay maker's directions. Allow the clay figure to cool completely.

3. **Paint the figure with brightly colored designs. Use a paper clip tip, cotton swabs, or toothpicks to add small details to your design. Wait for the paint to dry.**

4. **Cut 2 wings (4 inches long, or 10 cm) from the card stock, and decorate them to match your figure. Round the edges of the wings by curling the card stock over the edge of a table. Glue the base of each wing to the figure, and let it dry.**

5. **Cut your straws to 4 inches long (10 cm). Cut three evenly spaced, V-shaped notches in each straw. Make sure they run in a straight line down one side of the straw.**

© Disney

6.

6. Feed a 10-inch (25 cm) piece of string through each straw. A chopstick can help guide the string through. Secure the string by tying it through the first notch of the straw.

7. Glue the side of the straw without notches to each wing with the strings pointing down toward the body.

8. When the glue is dry, tie a loop at the end of the pieces of string. Holding your figure with one hand, place your pointer and middle finger into the two loops. Pull down to see the wings in action!

STEAM Takeaway

Creating moving wings for your figure may take more than one try. Can you think of ways to improve them? Testing different methods to find the best one is all part of the engineering process.

To Kiera, Kjell, Lene, and Magnus

Photo Acknowledgments

Additional image credits: Belozersky/Shutterstock.com (flask); E_K/Shutterstock.com (gears); Aksenova Natalya/Shutterstock.com (glue), p. 6; Olga Kovalenko/Shutterstock.com (scissors), p. 6; Lyudmila Suvorova/Shutterstock.com, p. 7; SJ Travel Photo and Video/Shutterstock.com (paints), p. 7.

Special thanks to content consultant Lars Ortiz

The photographs in this book were created by Shaina Olmanson.
Special thanks to hand models Anica, Tyonna, Trey, Brody, and Magnus.

Copyright © 2020 Disney Enterprises, Inc. and Pixar. All rights reserved.

No part of this book may be reproduced, stored in a retrieval system, or transmitted in any form or by any means—electronic, mechanical, photocopying, recording, or otherwise—without the prior written permission of Lerner Publishing Group, Inc., except for the inclusion of brief quotations in an acknowledged review.

Lerner Publications Company
A division of Lerner Publishing Group, Inc.
241 First Avenue North
Minneapolis, MN 55401 USA

For reading levels and more information, look up this title at www.lernerbooks.com.

Main body text set in Mikado a 14/18.
Typeface provided by HVD Fonts.

Library of Congress Cataloging-in-Publication Data

Names: Olmanson, Shaina, author.
Title: Coco idea lab / by Shaina Olmanson.
Description: Minneapolis : Lerner Publications, [2020] | Series: Disney STEAM projects | Includes bibliographical references and index. | Audience: Age 7–11. | Audience: K to Grade 3.
Identifiers: LCCN 2018054258 (print) | LCCN 2018055351 (ebook) | ISBN 9781541561564 (eb pdf) | ISBN 9781541554795 (lb : alk. paper) | ISBN 9781541574021 (pb : alk. paper)
Subjects: LCSH: Handicraft—Juvenile literature. | Science—Experiments—Juvenile literature. | Mexico—Social life and customs—Juvenile literature. | Coco (Motion picture)—Juvenile literature.
Classification: LCC TT160 (ebook) | LCC TT160 .O4585 2020 (print) | DDC 745.5—dc23

LC record available at https://lccn.loc.gov/2018054258

Manufactured in the United States of America
1-45797-42679-1/18/2019

© Disney